From Glory to Glory

A Study through 2 Corinthians

But we all, with unveiled face, beholding as in a mirror the glory of the Lord, are being transformed into the same image from glory to glory, just as by the Spirit of the Lord.

2 Corinthians 3:18

To be where God is will be glory.
To be what God intended will be glory.
To do what God purposed will be glory.

Introduction

The culminating reality of the new covenant is that it is a transforming covenant. That in the new covenant we look at the glory of the Lord revealed in the face of Jesus Christ unobstructed. We see Christ in all His wonder, in all His beauty and all His glory, as described in 2 Corinthians chapter 4 verse 6,

"Light shines out of darkness, the One who has shone in our hearts gives us the light of the knowledge of the glory of God in the face of Christ."

So as we look at the face of Christ we see the glory of God revealed. Nothing obscures us. We don't have a veil over our face like Moses did. There's nothing oblique or obscure, there's nothing hidden or dark or shadowy. The new covenant, the gospel, the message of Jesus Christ is clear. The light has been turned on and we can look with an unobstructed view right at the glory of God revealed in the face of Jesus Christ. And as we look at the glory of God and focus on the glory of God revealed in Christ, we are moved from one level of glory to the next by the Holy Spirit who is moving us into the image of the very glory we behold.

Now that poses, at least for me and I trust for you, a very practical question. If we say we are going to glorify God, we are going to aim at the glory of God, we are going to focus on the glory of God, we are going to gaze on the glory of God, we are going to glorify God with our lives...how do we do that? How do we really move from one level of glory to the next? What is specifically and practically involved in that?

John MacArthur

How do we really move from one level of glory to the next? What is specifically and practically involved in that? This study through 2 Corinthians seeks to answer these questions.

From Glory to Glory

How to Study

Welcome to "From Glory to Glory", a study through the Book of 2 Corinthians. Here are some suggestions to help you enjoy a daily, rich, satisfying time with God in His Word.

Before you begin each day, open your Bible and pray over the passage you will be reading. Allow your mind and heart to be opened to the teaching of the Holy Spirit.

Read through each week's passage out loud in its entirety from your Bible. Then focus on the selected scripture for each week by following the study format:

Beholding

This section of the study will open up the lesson focus and cause us to ponder and meditate upon the main idea of our passage.

Becoming

This section of the study will highlight the biblical principles to be learned, embraced and obeyed.

Reflecting

This section of the study applies what we have read and learned to our everyday life. With questions that will encourage and challenge our daily walk, this time is designed to move us on from glory to glory.

The more we behold Christ and stare deeply into His Word, the more we will become like Him, and reflect Him to a world that desperately needs Him.

When the people of God look into the Word of God and see the glory of God, the Spirit of God transforms them to be like the Son of God.

Warren Wiersbe

Study Lessons

The God of All Comfort

Lesson 1

Read 2 Corinthians chapter 1.
Focus on 2 Corinthians 1:3-7.

Blessed be the God and Father of our Lord Jesus Christ, the Father of mercies and God of all comfort, who comforts us in all our tribulation, that we may be able to comfort those who are in any trouble, with the comfort with which we ourselves are comforted by God. For as the sufferings of Christ abound in us, so our consolation also abounds through Christ. Now if we are afflicted, it is for your consolation and salvation, which is effective for enduring the same sufferings which we also suffer. Or if we are comforted, it is for your consolation and salvation. And our hope for you is steadfast, because we know that as you are partakers of the sufferings, so also you will partake of the consolation.

Lesson Focus - From Abundant Suffering to Abundant Comfort

By any estimation 2 Corinthians 1:3-7 frames the Bible's greatest text on comfort. The word "comfort" occurs no less than ten times in its noun and verb forms in this brief paragraph — essentially one-third of all thirty-one occurrences in the New Testament. Paul says more about suffering, and more about comfort, than any other writer in the Bible. And it is here that he says the most about it.

There is a reason for this, and it was to answer critics who held that the sufferings that characterized Paul's life were evidence that he was not an apostle, because if he was the real thing he wouldn't be experiencing so much trouble. Paul's answer was that abundant suffering and abundant comfort are in fact signs of apostolic authenticity.

R. Kent Hughes

Beholding

In her classic work, God of All Comfort, Hannah Whitall Smith describes in a very real way what is meant by the comfort of God.

But at this point I may be asked what I mean by the comfort God gives. Is it a sort of pious grace, that may perhaps fit us for Heaven, but that is somehow unfit to bear the brunt of our everyday life with its trials and its pains? Or is it an honest and genuine comfort, as we understand comfort, that enfolds life's trials and pains in an all-embracing peace?

With all my heart I believe it is the latter. Comfort, whether human or divine, is pure and simple comfort, and is nothing else. We, none of us, care for pious phrases, we want realities; and the reality of being comforted and comfortable seems to me almost more delightful than any other thing in life. We all know what it is. When as little children we have cuddled up into our mother's lap after a fall or a misfortune, and have felt her dear arms around us, and her soft kisses on our hair, we have had comfort. When, as grown-up people, after a hard day's work, we have put on our slippers and seated ourselves by the fire, in an easy chair with a book, we have had comfort. When, after a painful illness, we have begun to recover, and have been able to stretch our limbs and open our eyes without pain, we have had comfort. When someone whom we dearly love has been ill almost unto death, and has been restored to us in health again, we have had comfort.

A thousand times in our lives probably, have we said, with a sigh of relief, as a toil over or burdens laid down, "Well, this is comfortable," and in that word comfortable there has been comprised more a rest, and relief, and satisfaction, and pleasure, than any other word in the English language could possibly be made to express. We cannot fail, therefore, to understand the meaning of this name of God, the "God of all comfort".

1. Hannah describes the comfort of God as rest, relief and burdens laid down. How do the following scriptures support her description?

    - Psalm 4:1
    - Psalm 55:22
    - Matthew 11:28-30

2. Based on these verses, what are some ways we receive the comfort of God?

3. The word "comfort" comes from the Greek word "paraklesis". It appears ten times in 2 Corinthians 1:3-7, and is translated "comfort" six times and "consolation" four times. It combines the idea of solace with soothing.

    Look up the following words in a dictionary and compare their definitions.

    - Comfort
    - Consolation
    - Solace
    - Soothing

    How do these definitions help you to better understand the comfort of God?

4. We are never left to face sickness and sorrow alone. What does the "God of all comfort" say to His children in Isaiah 66:13?

5. The Lord compares His love and comfort to that of a mother. Can you remember a time from your childhood where your mother or a loving relative comforted you? Explain how their comfort helped you and provided a place of trust and security.

6. Describe Paul's experience in Asia in 2 Corinthians 1:8.

7. Identify a time in your life when you were…

   - Burdened beyond measure

   - Above strength (beyond all human ability or power to cope)

   - Despaired even of life

8. What important truth does Paul teach us about suffering in 2 Corinthians 1:9?

9. 2 Corinthians 1:10-11 reveals an important conclusion that Paul discovered about God in times of trouble. What conclusion did he come to and how does his testimony comfort you?

10. In 2 Corinthians 1:3 Paul also praises "the Father of mercies". Mercy is the outward manifestation of compassion for others in their affliction. Mercy had its origin with God, who is called its Father. All acts of pity and compassion proceed from Him. God has a tender feeling of compassion for us when we are in distress. Our trials, however slight or severe, have His attention.

    When we are being tested by adversity and affliction, compassion flows to us from God's great loving heart. What do we learn about the mercy of God from the following verses?

    - Psalm 103:13-14

    - Ephesians 2:4

    - Titus 3:5

No matter what variety of affliction we may be experiencing, and no matter what its intensity, God will provide strength and encouragement (comfort) that is adequate for our need. He will bestow more comfort than we have affliction. When scripture teaches that God is the God of ALL comfort, the word "ALL" means every kind, every variety, the whole of it, or the totality of the thing referred to. God's comfort is infinite, inexhaustible, immutable, and indestructible. Our afflictions are temporary and transient; but God's comfort is everlasting.

Write out 2 Thessalonians 2:16-17 and commit it to memory.

There are two things of which God is said to have the monopoly: He is 'the God of all grace' and He is 'the God of all comfort.' All grace comes from Him; all lasting comfort comes from Him.

Harry Ironside

Becoming

God does not comfort us to make us comfortable, but to make us comforters.

John Henry Jowett

God allows our suffering so that we are able to enter into others' suffering and offer comfort. In the New Testament the Greek word most frequently used for "comfort" is "paraklesis", which is closely related to the word "Paraclete", which describes the role of the Holy Spirit as Comforter. Like the Holy Spirit, we are called to "come alongside" those who are hurting and be present as a "helper".

1. Read Luke 10:25-37. The story of the Good Samaritan offers us a practical demonstration of the comfort of God. What can you take away from the passage to help you as you seek to be a comfort to others?

2. What severe trials or afflictions have you experienced and how have these equipped you to minister to others?

3. In 2 Corinthians 1:20 Paul passes on the beautiful truth that all the promises of God are true and trustworthy. God doesn't say one thing and mean another. If He promised, He will do it! It was Alan Redpath who said...

   A man who has believed God's promises and has said "Amen" to them in the depths of his soul without any hesitation, is a man to whose life had been communicated the divine character of the Holy Spirit.

   Alan Redpath

Standing on the promises I cannot fall,
Listening every moment to the Spirit's call
Resting in my Savior as my all in all,
Standing on the promises of God.

Alan Jackson

Consider some of the promises that are "YES" in Jesus Christ! There are so many but let's focus on a few that teach us about the certainty of God's heart toward us.

- What does God promise concerning His presence in Deuteronomy 31:6?

- What does God promise concerning His plans for you in Jeremiah 29:11?

- What does God promise concerning His forgiveness in Psalm 103:12?

- What does God promise concerning His love for you in Romans 8:37-39?

- What are some of the promises of God that have brought you comfort?

4. Share some practical ways you can use the promises of God to comfort others.

5. *The Romans marched in such a way that their shields would overlap. When attacked, they did not scatter. They stood strong together; they stayed in formation. This was a sign that made their opponents tremble because it made a statement: our ranks cannot be shaken. You are going down. Christians, stay in formation together. When you take up the shield of faith against the fiery darts of the evil one, lift the shields up together so that they are overlapping. In the midst of the fight, let us feel the mutuality of linking arms together so that we are in tune with one another in our battle song. Sometimes the song will be a song of mourning, sometimes it will be a song of jubilee. Let us stay in tune with one another so that what moves others to weep, moves us to weep as well. May what moves others to rejoice move us to rejoice as well.*

   Why is it so important to stay connected to one another in times of suffering?

You will have no test of faith that will not fit you to be a blessing if you are obedient to the Lord. I never had a trial but when I got out of the deep river I found some poor pilgrim on the bank that I was able to help by that very experience.

A. B. Simpson

Reflecting

1. When you are in need of God's comfort, what important truth can you rely upon in Psalm 116:2?

2. What do you learn about God's mercy and compassion from Lamentations 3:22, 23?

3. How should the knowledge of the comfort of God affect your attitude toward tribulation and suffering?

4. Share a time that God used another believer in your life to comfort you and demonstrate God's love and care for you.

5. Based on what you have learned today, in what ways can you glorify the God of all comfort by being a comfort to others?

6. Memorize 2 Corinthians 1:5 in the NLT and hide it in your heart.

For the more we suffer for Christ,
the more God will shower us with His comfort through Christ.

What comfort do you need from God today?
Sit and wait for him to visit you with His peace and reassurance.

The Transformed Life

Lesson 2

Read 2 Corinthians chapters 2&3.
Focus on 2 Corinthians 2:14-17.

Now thanks be to God who always leads us in triumph in Christ, and through us diffuses the fragrance of His knowledge in every place. For we are to God the fragrance of Christ among those who are being saved and among those who are perishing. To the one we are the aroma of death leading to death, and to the other the aroma of life leading to life. And who is sufficient for these things? For we are not, as so many, peddling the word of God; but as of sincerity, but as from God, we speak in the sight of God in Christ.

Lesson Focus - From Fleshly to Fragrant

There can be no question about the fragrance of Jesus. It was a part of His very nature. Wherever He went, whatever He did, whatever He said, the precious perfume of heaven accompanied Him. His human walk on earth was essentially one of communion with the Father. He never appeared before men without a lingering sweetness of the Sanctuary about Him. The fragrance of Christ is like the Father. It conveys the sweetness of the Father's love, the glory of the Father's character, the desirable loveliness of the Father's goodness. All that we can say is that this fragrance was the quality which brought the Presence of God to men. And all that we can say to describe the fragrance of a truly spiritual life is that it reminds men of Christ, it brings the atmosphere of His Presence near to men.

The lovely perfume of His life not only aroused longings and desires in men's hearts - it also seemed to inspire hope. Just as a sweet scent may inform us that there are beautiful flowers just beyond our sight, so this fragrant Son of Man suggested to the sons of men that God had something more for them if only they would press forward to receive it. Even in their defilement and bondage they were made to feel that there must be - there is - an answer from God. God is not afar off, distant and unmoved; He is very near, able and willing to impart His love and life to the needy. The fragrance did not heal them, but it made them draw near, it gave them new hope, it prepared the way for the ministry of healing. It made men feel that, if only they drew near enough, there would be a mighty provision from heaven to meet their deepest need.

Harry Foster

Beholding

I have a clear view of Jesus. I have seen Him, felt Him, and I have known Him in a far deeper way than simply by the outward physical appearance; I have felt the reality of His life begin to burn in my heart. I have seen in Christ the glory of a life that is totally submitted to the sovereignty of God. That glory has begun to take hold of me, and I have begun to see that this is the one life that God expects of any man He made in His own image. I have seen the marks of the cross upon Him, and by His grace the marks of the cross have been put upon me and I am no longer my own; I am bought with a price, redeemed by His precious blood. Yes, I have seen Him--not in the outward physical sense only, but in the inward sense of a deep spiritual reality. I have had a clear view of Jesus and my life will never be the same again.

Alan Redpath

The Scriptures have so much to impart to us about the fragrance of Christ. For the purpose of our study we will focus on 4 distinct fragrances.

1. *Read the verses below and describe the fragrance of Christ's love.*

   - John 3:16

   - Romans 5:8

   - Ephesians 5:1-2

   - Galatians 2:20

   - 1 John 4:10

2. *Read the verses below and describe the fragrance of Christ's forgiveness.*

   - Psalm 103:12

   - Ephesians 1:7

   - Hebrews 10:17

   - Colossians 1:13-14

3. *Read the verses below and describe the fragrance of Christ's holiness.*

- 2 Corinthians 5:21

- Hebrews 4:15

- Hebrews 7:26

It was customary in the Roman Empire after a major victory in battle to celebrate before the citizens of Rome with magnificent parades. As part of the ceremonies, people would throw fragrant flowers into the streets and as they were crushed beneath the feet of those in the procession it would fill the air with their fragrance. Even those that did not attend the parade could hear the music and smell the sweet aroma. They knew that Rome had been victorious. Christ delivered us from the stench of sin and death and rose in victory!

4. *Read the verses below and describe the fragrance of Christ's victory.*

- Matthew 28:18

- John 16:33

- 1 Corinthians 15:56-57

- Colossians 2:14-15

- 1 John 3:8

Becoming

We are to become the fragrance of Christ. We are not to be same Spirit filled Christian as the day we were saved. We are to progress from one degree or level of glory to another so that when we look into our spiritual mirrors we will see our continuing transformation; that of becoming more and more like Christ. We are never to remain the same, but to continue to shine more and more with the glory of God.

2 Corinthians 3:18 describes how we experience this transformation. Write out the verse.

As we behold Him we become like Him.

The word ***"beholding"*** *is in the present tense meaning a continuous beholding that is free from interruptions. The Christian steadfastly looks into the face of Jesus and reflects the glory of His face like a mirror reflecting light, and at the same time is continuously being transformed into the same image of Christ. We are being conformed to the image of Christ as we contemplate the glory of God on the face of Jesus. It is the process of sanctification. The more we behold this brilliant and glorious light, the more do we reflect back its rays; that is, the more we contemplate the great truths of the Christian religion, the more do our minds become imbued with its spirit. We are changed into His very image by a continued succession of Glory, as it were, streaming upon us from the Lord.*

Locke

1. In what ways does the Word of God help us to behold Him? Use Scripture to support your answer.

2. If we are abiding in Christ and living in the power of the Holy Spirit, the fruit of His Spirit will be evidenced in our life. What is the fruit of the Spirit described in Galatians 5:22-23?

3. Why are these characteristics so attractive to the world?

4. Are you growing in these Christ-like characteristics? Why or why not?

5. Which of these "fruits" would you like to grow in and why?

6. Read 2 Corinthians 3:13-18.

   Moses put a veil over his face so that the children of Israel could not look steadily at the end of what was passing away; ***his glow from being in the presence of God****. When Jewish people today refuse to accept the truth of the New Testament, we are told a veil continues to lie on their hearts. But the veil has been taken away in Christ and we behold Him with "unveiled faces". The glory of the Lord shining in us will never fade because of His Spirit which lives in us. If we are catching the glow in the time we spend with Jesus we will be reflecting it to the dark world around us.*

   Is any light getting through in your quiet time with Jesus? It may be the light is not getting through because you are not looking at Him long enough. How much time do you spend in the presence of God?

7. What other factors in our lives might prevent the light and fragrance of Christ from permeating in and through our lives?

8. 2 Corinthians 3:17 reveals an important truth – where the Spirit of the Lord is there is freedom. Christ freed us from the bondage of death and our hopeless efforts to obey the law by our own power. His Spirit gives us His life. We may say the right things, do the right things, give the right impression, but if we have lost touch with the Lord there will be no fragrance of Christ about us. This scent is not pungent, it is very delicate. It is easily lost; it cannot be produced or recovered by any effort of ours.

   John 15:4-5 provides us with the answer to protecting the life of Christ in us. What is it?

9. It has been said that we overcome ***not by inward struggle but by upward look***. What does it mean to "look up" when we encounter difficulty? Use Scripture to support your answer.

Reflecting

We cannot measure fragrance. Nor do we need to do so. It is altogether a matter of quality, not of quantity. The world in which we live is a world which tends to value everything according to its magnitude. Even in the realm of spiritual things we are all too prone to enquire first about dimensions, and to prize that which is big and impressive. Fragrance cannot be treated in this way. A very little scent can fill a whole room. A very small quantity can exert a widespread influence. God shows little interest in the things which seem so impressive to men. He is not asking us to be what the world calls 'big' or 'successful'. What He does seek is that which brings back to Him something of the sweet and satisfying perfume of the character of His Son. It is "to God", in the first place, that we are to be a sweet fragrance of Christ, and if we bring pleasure to God in our ministry, we shall undoubtedly bring blessing and life to men. We shall be a 'savour of life'.

Harry Foster

1. What do we discover in John 3:2 prompted Nicodemus to seek out Jesus?

2. Read Acts 4:13. What did the people notice about Peter and John as they addressed the Sanhedrin?

3. Share a time that people noticed "there was something different about you".

4. What does Paul mean in 2 Corinthians 3:2-3 when he compares us to an epistle that is known and read by all men?

5. What message does your life say to the world about Christ?

6. Paul teaches us that we are to diffuse the fragrance of Christ "in every place". Whether it be our homes, our neighborhoods, or our work places, our fragrance is not to be affected by our surroundings.

   Share a surrounding where you may feel uncomfortable in sharing your faith. What might help you overcome your hesitancy?

7. Our fragrance can be a deadly message for those who are unwilling to turn to Christ in faith. How are we to handle those who refuse our message? Use Scripture to support your answer.

8. There was something about Paul that made men long for a knowledge of God and at the same time fill them with the expectation that such a knowledge was possible. Matthew 5:13-16 would describe this quality as "saltiness".

   What are some of the properties of "salt" that help us to better understand "being salty"?

9. *Jesus did not have to try to be fragrant: it was a characteristic of His very inner nature that it gave forth the atmosphere of heaven. He has given this heavenly life to us. In our case also there is a sense in which we do not have to 'try' to be fragrant. We live out the life of the Lord Jesus, which carries with it everywhere the sweet scent of the character of God. To imitate it brings death, not life. To make any use of it other than for the glory of God alone, to seek some gain for ourselves out of it, also means bringing in death. We have the unique life within us. If only we can live it out, the fragrance will be found wherever we go.*

   Sum up what you have learned this week by writing a paragraph about the importance of "fragrance and radiance" in the life of the believer.

A mirror can only reflect what it sees. When the truth of the Word of God begins to dominate our character the life of Jesus Christ begins to be reproduced in us.

Turn your eyes upon Jesus
Look full in His wonderful face
And the things of the earth will grow strangely dim
In the light of His glory and grace

Lesson 3

Read 2 Corinthians chapter 4.
Focus on 2 Corinthians 4:7-12.

But we have this treasure in earthen vessels, that the excellence of the power may be of God and not of us. We are hard-pressed on every side, yet not crushed; we are perplexed, but not in despair; persecuted, but not forsaken; struck down, but not destroyed— always carrying about in the body the dying of the Lord Jesus, that the life of Jesus also may be manifested in our body. For we who live are always delivered to death for Jesus' sake, that the life of Jesus also may be manifested in our mortal flesh. So then death is working in us, but life in you.

Lesson Focus - From Despising our Weakness to Embracing It

The Tale of the Cracked Pot

A water bearer had two large pots, each hanging off the opposite end of a pole that he carried across his neck. One of the pots had a crack in it, and while the other pot was perfect and always delivered a full portion of water at the end of the long walk from the stream to the master's house, the cracked pot arrived only half full.

Of course, the perfect pot was proud of its accomplishments. But the poor cracked pot was ashamed of its own imperfection, and miserable that it was able to accomplish only half of what it had been made to do.

After two full years of what it perceived to be a bitter failure, it spoke to the water bearer one day by the stream. "I am ashamed of myself, and I want to apologize to you."

"Why?" asked the water bearer. "What are you ashamed of?"

The pot said, "I have been able, for these past two years, to deliver only half my load because this crack in my side causes water to leak out all the way back to your master's house. Because of my flaws, you have to do all of this work, and you don't get full value from your efforts."

The water bearer felt sorry for the cracked pot, and in his compassion he said, "As we return to the master's house, I want you to notice the beautiful flowers along the path."

Indeed, as they went up the hill, the cracked pot took notice of the beautiful flowers on the side of the path, and this cheered it some. But at the end of the trail, it still felt bad because it had leaked out half its load, and so again it apologized to the water bearer for its failure.

The bearer said to the pot, "Did you notice that there were flowers only on your side of the path, but not on the other pot's side? That's because I have always known about your flaw, and I worked with it. I planted flower seeds on your side of the path, and every day while we walk back from the stream, you've watered them. For years I have been able to pick these beautiful flowers to decorate my master's table. Without you being just the way you are, he would not have this beauty to grace his house.

We can all relate to the cracked pot. We are very aware of our imperfections, and to varying degrees we are ashamed of and even despise our weaknesses. When we recognize and understand our value by the treasure that lives within our containers, we begin to see the beauty of being wonderfully flawed and can actually live embracing our weaknesses. God uses His wonderfully flawed people to carry the greatest treasure the world has ever known.

Beholding

Clay jars were the throwaway containers of the ancient world, so that their life spans were generally a few years at the most. They were used to store and transport water and olive oil and wine and grain and even family treasures. Earthenware jars were an anonymous part of everyday living as they were used for cooking and eating and drinking and storing leftovers. Every domestic archaeological excavation site contains their remains, called ostraca, from the Greek word for pottery. No one took note of clay jars any more than we would of a fast-food container. They were simply there for convenience. It was no great tragedy when such vessels were broken. They were cheap and easy to replace.

1. We who believe in Christ are human containers. The true treasure is the glory of God in the person of Jesus, as presented and proclaimed by the **gospel**. Isaiah 52:7 provides us with insight into the meaning of the word "gospel". Write out the verse and record what you learn.

In a day of depressing headlines and uncertainty all around us, good news is very welcome. What better news could there be than as the old hymn says: "The vilest offender who truly believes, that moment from Jesus a pardon receives?" When Christians refer to the "Gospel" they are referring to the "good news" that Jesus Christ died to pay the penalty for our sin so that we might become the children of God through faith alone in Christ alone. In short, "the Gospel" is the sum total of the saving truth as God has communicated it to lost humanity as it is revealed in the person of His Son and in the Holy Scriptures, the Bible.

Bible.Org

2. It was John Piper who said:

   When you memorize a "gospel verse," and keep it warm, you have hidden in your heart a divinely inspired and inerrant expression, in human language, of the very point of the whole Bible and all of history. You carry with you the sword of the Spirit in its strongest alloy. One-sentence encapsulations of the Bible's central message strengthen our spiritual backbone and solidify our core, rooting us deep down in the bedrock of God's heart and the nature of the world He made, and sending us into confident combat with unbelief, whether our own or someone's else. "Gospel verses" are invaluable in both evangelism and discipleship.

   Look up the following "gospel verses" and describe the treasure found in each one.

   - Mark 10:45
   - Romans 5:8
   - Romans 6:23
   - Romans 8:1
   - Romans 8:32
   - 2 Corinthians 5:21
   - 2 Corinthians 8:9
   - 1 Timothy 1:15
   - 1 John 4:10
   - Revelation 5:9

3. **The Gospel in a Nutshell**

   Read 1 Corinthians 15:1-8. In these verses the apostle Paul summarizes the most basic ingredients of the gospel message, namely, the death, burial, resurrection, and appearances of the resurrected Christ. Underline the word "**that**" in the following verses and then circle the gospel truth that follows.

   - **1 Corinthians 15:3**

     For I delivered to you first of all that which I also received: that Christ died for our sins according to the Scriptures

   - **1 Corinthians 15:4**

     And that He was buried, and that He rose again the third day according to the Scriptures,

   - **1 Corinthians 15:5**

     And that He was seen by Cephas, then by the twelve.

4. The fact that God offers us salvation as a free gift through faith in Christ is good news beyond description. How does Paul link the gospel with faith in Galatians 3:6-9?

5. If the salvation offered to us were dependent on our merit or our ability to keep the law, it would not be good news because of our sinfulness and complete inability to keep the law or any kind of righteous principles as a means of our justification or right standing with God. Go deeper into this truth by recording what you discover in the following verses:

   - Romans 3:19-20

   - Galatians 2:16

6. What do we learn about grace and salvation in Ephesians 2:8-9?

7. What do we learn about the "treasure" of the gospel in Romans 1:16?

8. We should not be ashamed of the gospel of Christ, for it is the power of God to save everyone who believes! Because of what Jesus Christ accomplished for you on the cross, the Bible states "He that has the Son has life." You can receive the Son, Jesus Christ, as your Savior by personal faith, by trusting in the person of Christ and His death for your sins.

   What do you learn about receiving Christ in John 1:12 and John 3:16-18?

9. We each come to God the same way:

   - *As a sinner who recognizes her sinfulness*
   - *As a sinner who realizes no human works can save her*
   - *As a sinner who relies totally on Christ alone by faith alone for salvation*

If you would like to receive and trust Christ as your personal Savior, you may want to express your faith in Christ by a simple prayer acknowledging your sinfulness, accepting His forgiveness and putting your faith in Christ for your salvation. Share your decision with your small group leader or another Christian. If you have already made a decision for Christ, share the time you first placed your trust in Him.

Becoming

Both God and the Gospel gain glory from the weakness of the vessels in which they are contained. Weakness means we don't have what it takes. It means we are neither sovereign nor omniscient, nor invincible. We are not in control, we don't know everything, and we can be stopped. Weakness means that we desperately need God. And the plea for my own soul, and for yours, is that we would embrace weakness, not despise it.

Jonathan Parnell – Desiring God

1. We see in the culture a celebration of strength, independence and self-sufficiency. How are the truths found in 1 Corinthians 1:26-31 completely contrary to the culture?

2. Why did God choose the weak things of the world to put to shame the things that are mighty?

3. How can depending on our own strength rob us of the power of God?

When we embrace weakness, it means we've looked at ourselves long enough to know we can't make it without looking to Another. Embracing weakness means admitting how much we need God.

4. It is during times of difficulty and hardship that we are weak and vulnerable. Describe Paul's attitude toward hardship in 2 Corinthians 4:8-9.

- Hard-pressed on every side, yet not__________________________________.
- Perplexed but not in ____________________________________.
- Persecuted but not______________________________________.
- Struck down but not_____________________________________.

5. Share a situation that caused you to feel "hard pressed," "perplexed," "persecuted," or "struck down."

6. Paul knew the power and victory of Jesus in his life because he was continually in situations where only the power and victory of Jesus could meet his need! Read Acts 14:19-20 and describe the power of God working in Paul's weakness.

7. In our weakness, it can be easy to "lose heart" when trials come upon us. You may be surprised to discover that meaning behind the Greek word for "lose heart" is "faint-hearted coward." The Greek word implies not only a lack of courage but of bad behavior and evil conduct.

   In what ways can our response to suffering work against the glory of God?

8. Paul wanted the life of Jesus in him to be evident to all. But Paul knew this could only happen if he carried about in his body the dying of the Lord Jesus. There are some aspects of God's great work in our lives that only happen through trials and suffering. But for Paul, every death-like trial was just the prelude to resurrection power!

   Christ died that we might live. The great exchange of the gospel is: Christ's life for ours. And those who are used most to spread the good news of Christ embrace death as the operational principle of ministry. When George Muller, pastor and provider for thousands of children, was asked his secret, he hung his head and said, "There was a day when I died." Then he hung it lower and said, "Died to George Muller."

   R. Kent Hughes

   To embrace weakness, we must die to our will so that Christ's purposes can be accomplished through our suffering. As Jesus approached His death on the cross, His words in the garden must be also be ours:

   Write out Luke 22:42.

9. To embrace weakness, we must die to our will so that Christ's purposes can be accomplished through our suffering. How does Jesus help us to better understand this principle "of dying" in John 12:24-26?

Reflecting

1. How has "the god of this age" (2 Corinthians 4:4) blinded the minds of unbelievers? What is the evidence of this all around us?

2. We see from our text that it can be easy to lose heart. What are some of the things that have caused you to lose heart in walking with Christ and serving Him?

3. Why is it important to keep the truth of 2 Corinthians 4:14 ever before us?

4. Read 2 Corinthians 4:13-15. Faith is essential to every area of the Christian life? Paul believed, therefore he spoke. Are you able to stand up and declare your faith? Why or why not?

5. What does Paul tell us in 2 Corinthians 4:16-18 that we need to remember when we begin to lose heart?

6. Contrast the words that Paul uses in 2 Corinthians 4:16-18.

   - Outward vs. Inward

   - Perishing vs. Renewed

   - Light and Momentary vs. Eternal

   - The Seen vs. the Unseen

7. Based on what you have learned, write a paragraph explaining what it means to live in this world with an eternal perspective.

If I find in myself a desire which no experience in this world can satisfy,
the most probable explanation is that I was made for another world.

C.S. Lewis

The Judgment Seat of Christ

Lesson 4

Read 2 Corinthians chapter 5.
Focus on 2 Corinthians 5:9-11.

Therefore we make it our aim, whether present or absent, to be well pleasing to Him. For we must all appear before the judgment seat of Christ, that each one may receive the things done in the body, according to what he has done, whether good or bad. Knowing, therefore, the terror of the Lord, we persuade men; but we are well known to God, and I also trust are well known in your consciences.

Lesson Focus - From Running to Winning

The hit movie Gladiator begins with a powerful scene. Just before engaging the German barbarians in battle, General Maximus addresses some of his Roman soldiers. "Brothers," he says, "what we do in life echoes in eternity." Although Maximus was a pagan, his statement is entirely consistent with biblical Christianity, particularly the Bible's teaching on eternal rewards.

While salvation is a gift, there are rewards given for faithfulness in the Christian life and loss of rewards for unfaithfulness. We are not merely in this race to run, but to win!

Paul said it perfectly in 1 Corinthians 9:24-25:

Do you not know that those who run in a race all run, but one receives the prize? Run in such a way that you may obtain it. And everyone who competes for the prize is temperate in all things. Now they do it to obtain a perishable crown, but we for an imperishable crown.

Beholding

The Lord is absolutely worthy of our obedience and service, whether we ever personally profit from it or not. Nevertheless, the Lord is a rewarder of those who seek Him and He commands us to seek His rewards as well! And when we really think about it, "Hearing our Master say, 'Well done' will not simply be for our pleasure but for His!"

Randy Alcorn

1. Before approaching the topic of rewards and the judgment seat of Christ, Paul first speaks to what should be our aim and motivation in the Christian life. What is the goal Paul lays out for us in 2 Corinthians 5:9?

2. Pleasing the Lord should be the great ambition of every believers' heart. Kay Smith, in her book, Pleasing God provides us with further insight.

   To please someone means to delight, to satisfy, or to gratify. When our aim is to please God, then we begin to weigh all our actions in the light of whether or not those actions are pleasing to Him. And this is not something we do just out of obedience. We do these things out of an attitude of love. There is a big difference between the two. If you have children, you know that they can obey you by taking out the trash, while griping all the way. But if one morning the trash has been emptied just to please you, you know the difference – and God does too.

   What do the following verses teach us about pleasing God?

   - Romans 8:8

   - Galatians 1:10

   - Colossians 1:10

   - 2 Timothy 2:4

   - Hebrews 11:6

3. Based upon what you have learned, write in your own words what it means to live a life that is pleasing to God.

4. The Judgment Seat of Christ will be a crowning day for those Christians who will receive rewards for their works. Unlike the laurel and ivy crowns received from officials at the Bema seat of the Olympics in Corinth, the child of God will receive eternal crowns from the Lord Jesus Himself. (John 5:22).

   Paul is picturing the believer as a competitor in a spiritual contest. As the victorious Grecian athlete appeared before the Bema to receive his perishable reward, so the Christian will appear before Christ's Bema to receive his imperishable reward. It is important to note that this is a time of rewards or loss of rewards following examination of a believer's life, not a time of punishment where believers are judged for their sins.

   Revelation 22:12 confirms this truth in Jesus' own words. What does He say?

5. The New Testament describes as many as five different crowns which will be given to believers for various works of faithfulness, obedience, discipline, and love. Look up each Scripture and draw a line connecting the appropriate crown with its rewarded behavior.

CROWN	**WORKS**
The Imperishable Crown (1 Corinthians 9:25)	Faithfulness to Christ in persecution or martyrdom
The Crown of Rejoicing (Philippians 4:1, 1 Thessalonians 2:19)	Determination, discipline and victory in the Christian life
The Crown of Righteousness (2 Timothy 4:8)	Faithfully representing Christ in a position of leadership
The Crown of Glory (1 Peter 5:4)	Pouring oneself into others in evangelism and discipleship
The Crown of Life (Revelation 2:10, James 1:12)	To all who long for His appearing

Becoming

1. What did Jesus tell His followers in the Sermon on the Mount in Matthew 6:19-21?

2. Read 1 Corinthians 3:9-15.

   Paul illustrates the sober reality that some Christians will be resurrected with precious little to show for the time they spent on earth—they "will be saved, but only as one escaping through the flames." This conjures up images of people escaping burning buildings with little more than the charred clothes upon their backs. This will be the lot of even the most visible Christian leaders whose motives were selfish rather than selfless. Conversely, those who build selflessly upon the foundation of Christ using "gold, silver and costly stones" will receive enduring rewards.

   Give some examples of the works of a believer that will burn and suffer loss.

3. Our works are what we have done with our resources – time, energy, talents, money, and possessions. What are you doing with the resources that God has entrusted to you to build His kingdom?

4. Jesus indicates in Matthew 12:36 that words, even carelessly spoken words, are eternally important. We will be held accountable for "every idle word". James echoes Jesus' emphasis on the crucial importance of the use of words in daily life. What do you learn about the tongue in James 3:1-12?

5. What are some ways we can use our words to glorify God? Use Scripture to support your answer.

Reflecting

1. Explain what is meant in 2 Corinthians 5:5 by the truth "that God has given us the Spirit as a guarantee?

2. How should this guarantee help us not to merely run our race, but win it?

3. What important truth does Paul reveal in 2 Corinthians 5:14-15?

4. Is your love for Christ compelling you to live for Him? Why or why not?

5. The Crown of Rejoicing will be given to those who poured themselves out for evangelism and discipleship. Paul makes it clear in 2 Corinthians 5:18 and 20 that every believer has a ministry of reconciliation and serves as an ambassador for Christ.

   Describe what it means to be a minister of reconciliation and an ambassador for Christ.

6. What are some ways you be intentional about running your race to win?

7. Are there any areas in your life which are less than pleasing to God? What will you do today to change that?

Above Reproach

Lesson 5

Read 2 Corinthians chapter 6.
Focus on 2 Corinthians 6:1-10.

We then, as workers together with Him also plead with you not to receive the grace of God in vain. For He says:

"In an acceptable time I have heard you,
And in the day of salvation I have helped you."
Behold, now is the accepted time; behold, now is the day of salvation.

We give no offense in anything, that our ministry may not be blamed. But in all things we commend ourselves as ministers of God: in much patience, in tribulations, in needs, in distresses, in stripes, in imprisonments, in tumults, in labors, in sleeplessness, in fastings; by purity, by knowledge, by longsuffering, by kindness, by the Holy Spirit, by sincere love, by the word of truth, by the power of God, by the armor of righteousness on the right hand and on the left, by honor and dishonor, by evil report and good report; as deceivers, and yet true; as unknown, and yet well known; as dying, and behold we live; as chastened, and yet not killed; as sorrowful, yet always rejoicing; as poor, yet making many rich; as having nothing, and yet possessing all things.

Lesson Focus – From Walking to Witness

The dictionary defines "reproach" as shame or disgrace, or that which brings rebuke or censure upon a person. For Paul, this person was Christ. He was absolutely resolute in his determination that he would bring no shame or disgrace to his ministry or Christ. "Above reproach" does not mean that we live without sin. It does mean that we try to live in such a way that no one will be hindered from finding the Lord by the way we act, so no one can find fault with our ministry. This chapter in 2 Corinthians should inspire and challenge us as Christians to not merely walk daily with Christ, but to witness and serve Him without compromise.

Beholding

God's grace is always coming to my heart and life in the very wonderful and blessed experience of now. Yesterday's grace is totally inadequate for the burden of today, and if I do not learn to lay hold of heavenly resources every day of my life for the little things as well as the big things, as a Christian I soon become stale, barren, and fruitless in the service of the Lord.

Alan Redpath

Paul challenged the Corinthians to "not to receive the grace of God in vain" but to accept and live in the freedom of grace and making sacrifices—so that they neither squander the gift through unrighteous living or fail to make it attractive to others.

1. Define God's grace in your own words and explain why you are grateful for His amazing grace.

2. To help you better appreciate God's grace, make a list of those things He has given you that you did not deserve.

3. Read 2 Corinthians 6:1. The phrase "in vain" means "without effect or result." Paul's concern is that God's grace will not have any meaningful impact on the Corinthian's lives. It was Frederick William Faber (English hymn writer) who said, *"God does not save us by grace so that we may live in disgrace."*

   Look up the following verses and make note of what it means to take the grace of God in vain.

   - Romans 6:1-2

   - 1 Corinthians 15:10

   - Galatians 2:21

   - James 2:26

   - Jude 4

If God is going to give you His grace and power, then He is going to want you to do something with it. Too many Christians are sitting in the dugout refusing to get into the real game of life with the Lord. God can give you the baseball bat – which represents His gifts, grace, and power – but you have to be willing to step out of the dugout and get up to the plate and use the power of that bat to hit the ball. If you do not, then all of God's gifts, grace, and power that He was wanting to give to you in the first place will all end up being wasted, and you will end up receiving His grace in vain since you did absolutely nothing with the grace that He had initially given to you – just like Paul is perfectly describing in this passage –

Bible Knowledge Commentary

4. Have you stepped out of the dugout and into the game? Why or why not?

5. Paul speaks in 2 Corinthians 6:2 to the urgency of now – *today is the day of salvation.* Paul would have been concerned for those who were in the Corinthian church that were not saved. How can you show the same concern for those in your church who may not be saved?

6. Think of someone you know who is unsaved. Take a moment to pray that he or she will respond to the grace of God and receive the gift of salvation through Jesus Christ.

Becoming

Never reserve anything. Pour out the best you have, and always be poor. Never be diplomatic and careful about the treasure God gives. This is poverty triumphant.

Oswald Sanders

Paul ascribes great importance to an intentionally faithful witness for the presence and power of the Lord God through His Holy Spirit in a believer's daily walk.

1. Read 2 Corinthians 6:3-4(a) taken from the New Living Translation.

   We live in such a way that no one will stumble because of us, and no one will find fault with our ministry. In everything we do, we show that we are true ministers of God.

   Like Paul, we too want to be a faithful witness for Christ. What are some ways we can avoid life choices which misrepresent Christ?

2. Describe the difficulties that Paul faced in 2 Corinthians 6:4-5.

3. Paul faced these difficulties with much "patience". In the NT the word "patience" describes the characteristic of a man who is not swerved from his deliberate purpose and his loyalty to faith and piety by even the greatest trials and sufferings (Blue Letter Bible).

   The word used in the original language of the New Testament is "hupomone", which has the idea of endurance instead of simply waiting. We often think of patience as a passive thing – the ability to sit around and wait for something to happen. That is not the idea of the word Paul uses here. It is an active endurance instead of a passive waiting. The Greek word "hupomone" does not describe the frame of mind which can sit down with folded hands and bowed head and let a torrent of troubles sweep over it in passive resignation. It describes the ability to bear things in such a triumphant way that it transfigures them." (Barclay)

   How might Paul's endurance in times of great hardship attract the attention of unbelievers?

4. Share a time of difficulty in your life where the people around you could not comprehend your patience and peace.

5. Write out 2 Peter 1:3.

6. In 2 Corinthians 6:6-7, make a list of the resources Paul took advantage of in triumphing over adversity. How can you use these divine resources to overcome trials in your life?

7. The world (including the worldly Corinthian Christians) described Paul with words like: dishonor, evil report, deceivers, unknown, dying, chastened, sorrowful, poor, having nothing. *God described Paul with words like*: honor, good report, true, well known, behold we live, not killed, always rejoicing, making many rich, possessing all things.

   Are you more concerned with the way the world sees you or the way that God sees you? Explain your answer.

Reflecting

Paul's challenge then and ours today is to "not become partners with those who do not believe", we are given a clear command in 2 Corinthians 6:14 to not be unequally yoked with unbelievers.

1. Read 2 Corinthians 6:11-13. Paul loved the Corinthian church with the heart of a father. He lived out the truth of Ephesians 4:15. What truth did he put into practice?

2. Do you find it difficult to be open and honest with other believers? Why or why not?

3. There were still those in the church who were not over the rebuke Paul had to deliver in 1 Corinthians. Paul had forgiven the Corinthians and opened his heart to them, but they were closing their heart to him. If there was to be true reconciliation, they also had to be open. What influence should Paul's love have had on the Corinthians?

4. In 2 Corinthians 6:14-18, Paul is speaking to the overly broad affections of the Corinthian Christians. They had joined themselves to unbelievers, and this was affecting their reconciliation with Paul. What are some ways Christians seek to excuse unequally yoked relationships whether in business or romance?

5. To get a better idea of what the word "yoked" means, look up the definitions of the following words:

    - Fellowship
    - Communion
    - Accord
    - Part
    - Agreement

6. Based on these definitions what does it mean to not "yoke" yourself with an unbeliever?

7. Fill in the blanks from 2 Corinthians 6:14-15.

    - For what **fellowship** has ________________________ with ______________?
    - And what **communion** has ________________________ with ______________?
    - And what **accord** has ____________________________with ______________?
    - Or what **part** has a ________________________________with an___________?
    - And what **agreement** has the __________ _____ ________ with____________?

8. 2 Corinthians 6:16 explains why we are not to be yoked together with unbelievers. What is it?

9. What are the repercussions to Christ's reputation when we yoke ourselves to unbelievers?

10. Commentator David Guzik gives great insight regarding this passage of Scripture. Read his comments and then take an inventory of your own life.

Paul means much more here than only marrying an unbeliever. It really applies to any environment where we let the world influence our thinking. When we are being conformed to this world and are not being transformed by the renewing of our mind (Romans 12:2), we are joining together with unbelievers in an ungodly way.

This speaks especially to the issue of influence. Paul is not suggesting that Christians never associate with unbelievers (he makes this clear in 1 Corinthians 5:9-13). The principle is that we are to be in the world, but not of the world, like a ship should be in the water, but water shouldn't be in the ship! But if the world is influencing us, it is clear we are unequally yoked together with unbelievers. And this unequal yoke, or ungodly influence, may come through a book, a movie, a television show, a magazine, or even through worldly Christian friends. Most Christians are far too indiscriminate about the things they allow to influence their minds and lives.

We all like to believe that we can be around ungodly things as much as we want, and that we are strong enough to ward off the influence. But we must take seriously the words of Scripture: Do not be deceived: "Evil company corrupts good habits" (1 Corinthians 15:33). It needs to come back to the simple question from Romans 12:2: are we being conformed to this world or are we being transformed by the renewing of your mind?

The Corinthian Christians were thinking like worldly people, not like godly people. They gained this way of looking at life - or at least stayed in it - because of their ungodly associations. Paul tells them to break those yokes of fellowship with the ungodly!

Take a moment to pause and consider if there is any area in your life where you are "attaching" yourself to the world.

Lesson 6

Read 2 Corinthians chapter 7.
Focus on 2 Corinthians 7:9-11.

Now I rejoice, not that you were made sorry, but that your sorrow led to repentance. For you were made sorry in a godly manner, that you might suffer loss from us in nothing. For godly sorrow produces repentance leading to salvation, not to be regretted; but the sorrow of the world produces death. For observe this very thing, that you sorrowed in a godly manner: What diligence it produced in you, what clearing of yourselves, what indignation, what fear, what vehement desire, what zeal, what vindication! In all things you proved yourselves to be clear in this matter.

Lesson Focus – From Sorrow to Repentance

In this week's study we find one of the most enlightening passages in the New Testament on the important subject of repentance. Paul makes a distinct separation between sorrow and repentance. It is possible for a believer to be sorry for their sin without repenting from their sin. Sorrow describes a feeling, but repentance describes a change in both the mind and the life.

Godly sorrow that leads to repentance, therefore, is a sorrow that leads to a change of purpose, of intention, and of action. It is not the sorrow of idle tears; it is not crying by your bedside because once again you have failed; nor is it vain regret, wishing things had never happened, wishing you could live the moments again. No, it is not that. It is a change of purpose and intentions, a change of direction and action.

Alan Redpath

Beholding

1. What were some of the sin issues in the Corinthian church that Paul had to deal with?

    - 1 Corinthians 3:1-4

    - 1 Corinthians 5:1-8

    - 1 Corinthians 6:1-8

2. In light of the sin in the church, why was it important for Paul to address these issues and call for the church's repentance?

Many people are offended by the word "repentance", but when we truly understand it in the fullness of its gospel intention, it is a beautiful word that invites healing and freedom.

3. What did John the Baptist preach in Matthew 3:2?

4. What did Jesus preach in Matthew 4:17?

5. What did Peter preach in Acts 2:38?

The Greek word used for repentance in the New Testament is "metanoia" which means to change one's mind. Specifically, repentance is a change of mind about sin and about God, which results in turning from sin to God.

6. Write out Romans 2:4.

7. What is it about the goodness of God that should lead us to repentance? Use Scripture to support your answer.

8. True repentance will lead to a *sorrowing* for sin, a *confessing* of sin and *forsaking* of sin. Read Psalm 51 and cite the verses that point to David's true repentance.

   - Sorrowing for sin

   - Confessing sin

   - Forsaking sin

Becoming

Therefore, having these promises, beloved, let us cleanse ourselves from all filthiness of the flesh and spirit, perfecting holiness in the fear of God.

2 Corinthians 7:1

When we seek forgiveness, God is faithful and just to forgive us our sins and to cleanse us from all unrighteousness, but God will not do for us what we must do for ourselves. Only we can put out of our lives those things that defile us, and we know what they are. We must separate ourselves from whatever defiles us and grieves the Father.

Warren Wiersbe

1. Take a moment to consider the music you listen to, the movies you watch, the internet sites you visit, the books you read, and the relationships you are engaged in. Is there anything that you need to separate yourself from? Explain your answer.

2. Consider C. S. Lewis' comment from Mere Christianity on sins of the flesh and sins of the spirit.

   The sins of the flesh are bad, but they are the least bad of all sins. All the worst pleasures are purely spiritual: the pleasure of putting other people in the wrong, of bossing and patronizing and spoiling sport, and back-biting, the pleasures of power, of hatred. For there are two things inside me, competing with the human self which I must try to become. They are the Animal self, and the Diabolical self. The Diabolical self is the worse of the two. That is why a cold, self-righteous prig who goes regularly to church may be far nearer to hell than a prostitute. But, of course, it is better to be neither.

How would you explain the difference between sins of the flesh and sins of the spirit?

3. Read 2 Corinthians 7:2-4 in the Phillips translation.

   Do make room in your hearts again for us! Not one of you has ever been wronged or ruined or cheated by us. I don't say this to condemn your attitude, but simply because, as I said before, whether we live or die you live in our hearts. To your face I talk to you with utter frankness; behind your back I talk about you with deepest pride. Whatever troubles I have gone through, the thought of you has filled me with comfort and deep happiness.

   What is Paul's heart toward the believer's in Corinth? How should they have responded to his message?

4. Read 2 Corinthians 7:5-16. It's not easy to confront sin in the life of another believer and Paul recognized that. Though he did cause the Corinthians to sorrow about their sin, he did it in a godly way. He used the truth, not lies or exaggeration. He was honest, not using hidden agendas and manipulation. He simply told the truth in love.

   Do you have a hard time receiving the truth in love? Why or why not?

5. Sorrow in itself doesn't produce anything except bad feelings. But godly sorrow produces repentance. Since repentance is a change (in both thinking and action), we can tell if sorrow is really godly by seeing if it produces repentance. So godly sorrow cannot be measured by feelings or tears, but by what it produces.

   In Genesis 25:27–34, Esau presents us with an example of the power of the flesh when he chose the bowl of stew over his birthright. He chose the temporal over the eternal. He despised his birthright and considered it of no more value than a single meal. Esau returns from the hunt to receive his blessing to discover that the blessing has already been given to Jacob. Esau then begins to weep, yet his sorrow is worldly sorrow, not godly. He weeps only for himself and the consequences he will suffer. His sorrow is not one that leads to repentance, but one that comes from selfishness and leads only to death.

   What is the warning we receive in Hebrews 12:14-17?

Reflecting

Paul had made several visits to Corinth and also written several letters, only two of which are preserved for us in the New Testament. Having read all the letters Paul has written to them, the Corinthians immediately understand what he is talking about when he refers to the "sorrowful letter."

That letter was sorrowful because it caused both Paul and the Corinthians to sorrow. Paul had his regrets in sending this letter, because he knew at the time the pain it would cause them. He no more enjoyed causing them pain by this letter than a parent enjoys watching a child suffer when he or she must be spanked. But he also knew that there was no other way to deal with their sin other than to expose and confront it with a letter of rebuke. Paul's sorrow turns to joy when he learns that his sorrowful letter produced its desired effect—repentance on the part of the Corinthians.

1. Paul describes in detail in 2 Corinthians 7:11 what godly sorrow produces in the life of a believer. List the 7 characteristics of godly sorrow mentioned here and give an example of each.

2. Read 2 Corinthians 7:16. How do we know that Paul believed the Corinthian's repentance was genuine?

True love is willing to rebuke when it is required by sin, but it is willing to believe the very best when a wayward sinner repents and seeks to return to fellowship with God's people.

3. How did Paul demonstrate the instruction we receive in Galatians 6:1 and James 5:19-20?

4. Far too many Christians today are walking around with things hidden in their heart that are eating them alive spiritually. Unconfessed sins break down our faith, destroy our confidence in Christ, and rob us of our peace and joy. Not to mention, unrepented sin can cause a whole flurry of spiritual problems in our lives.

   Proverbs 16:18 reveals one of the biggest obstacles to repentance. What is it?

5. Is pride getting in the way of true repentance in your life? Is there someone you need to forgive or ask forgiveness from?

6. What is the most important thing you have learned about true repentance in studying 2 Corinthians chapter 7. How will you take what you have learned and put it into practice?

Lesson 7

Read 2 Corinthians chapters 8& 9.
Focus on 2 Corinthians 9:6-8.

But this I say: He who sows sparingly will also reap sparingly, and he who sows bountifully will also reap bountifully. So let each one give as he purposes in his heart, not grudgingly or of necessity; for God loves a cheerful giver. And God is able to make all grace abound toward you, that you, always having all sufficiency in all things, may have an abundance for every good work.

Lesson Focus – From Giving to Generosity

Paul was encouraging the church in Corinth to give a financial gift to support the struggling Christians in Jerusalem. These Jewish believers were facing severe financial consequences because of their faith. Paul appealed to the generosity of the Corinthians on the basis of "God's indescribable gift". He reminds believers then and us today that after what God had done for us, generosity toward each other should come easily. This portion of scripture gives us the most comprehensive instruction in the Bible on the practical subject of giving and introduces us to the very important principle of sowing and reaping. The examples, guidelines and principles in this week's lesson should inspire, motivate and enable us to abound in the grace of giving!

Beholding

1. It is important as we study "giving" that we begin with Paul's concluding words to the Corinthian church in 2 Corinthians 9:15. Write them out!

2. Paul expresses his appreciation to the greatest Giver of all! What do we learn about God's indescribable gift from Romans 8:32?

3. Reflect on this statement, "thanks be to God for his indescribable gift". What is it about this gift that makes it indescribable?

4. What should be our motivation for giving that we read in 2 Corinthians 8:9?

Though God was rich, in the glory and honor that was eternally His in heaven, He became poor. He gave up His heavenly glory and came to earth to live as a man and to suffer and die. Our response should be nothing less than giving of ourselves for the sake of others.

5. What does James 1:17 tell us about God and His gifts?

6. Read 2 Corinthians 8:1-5. In what ways are the Macedonians excellent examples of generosity?

7. Compare the giving of the Macedonians with the giving of the widow in Luke 21:1-4.

8. Reflect on your own pattern of giving. When is it hard for you to give?

9. In both chapters Paul refrains from using the word *money*. Instead he uses words like *sharing*, *service*, *offering*, *grace* and *gift*. What insights do these words give us into the nature of giving?

10. Paul never raised money for himself, for his own missionary organization or even for Corinth Community Church. What do you learn about the heart of giving in 2 Corinthians 8:10-15?

11. What care does Paul take to avoid any suspicion of dishonesty or self-interest as he handles this large gift in 2 Corinthians 8:16-24?

12. Some people teach that giving money to the Lord's work results in your getting more money yourself. What does Paul say about the personal benefits of giving in 2 Corinthians 9:6-11?

Becoming

Paul refers to giving money as a grace. The fact that Paul would use the Greek word "charis" to describe financial giving means a few things. David Guzik pinpoints this idea perfectly.

The ability to give and the heart to give is a free gift from God. Giving is a work of God's grace in us. When you see a believer who is truly generous, a great work of God has been done in their heart. We should never say, "Well, they just want to write the checks and not get involved." No; giving is getting involved, and it demonstrates a true work of God's grace in the heart.

Our giving should be like God's giving of grace to us: giving freely, generously, because we want to give. When God gives to us out of grace, the motive for His giving is in Him, not based in the one receiving. That is how we should give; because the motive of the love and generosity of God is so big in our heart that we simply must give.

Our giving, like God's grace to us, should be offered without expectation of payment in return. God does not give to us expecting "payback." We can never repay God. We can just serve Him and love Him in return.

Once you see the matter of giving is centered in this lovely word grace, it lifts the whole act away from mechanics, from pressure and duty, from obligation and mere legalism. It lifts us up into the most lovely atmosphere of an activity which seeks by giving to convey to others all that is lovely, all that is beautiful, all that is good, and all that is glorious. What a lovely word this word is . . . For there is no area in the Christian life in which grace shines out so much, so beautifully, so delightfully, and so happily as when giving comes from the background of poverty. (Redpath)

1. Based on what you have just learned, do you think that you have fully embraced the grace of giving? Why or why not?

2. In 2 Corinthians 9:6 Paul uses a natural law in agriculture to illustrate an important spiritual principle. Think about this as you fill in the missing words from 2 Corinthians 9:6.

   - She who sows ____________________ will also reap ____________________
   - She who sows ____________________will also reap ____________________

3. Define the following words

   - Sow
   - Reap
   - Sparingly
   - Bountifully

4. What do you learn about sowing and reaping from the following verses?

   Proverbs 11:24-25

   Malachi 3:10

   Luke 6:38

5. Read Galatians 6:6-10. The principle of sowing and reaping goes beyond monetary giving. What do you discover?

Every choice has a consequence. If we make wise, godly decisions, we can expect the Lord to reward us for our faithfulness. If we make rash or sinful choices, we can anticipate negative consequences. The fruit—good or bad—is usually not evident immediately. But one day, we will either be rewarded for righteous living or reap the consequences for rebellion against God.

Charles Stanley

6. Give some examples of sowing to the Spirit and sowing to the flesh.

7. Unfortunately false teachers have greatly distorted the biblical teaching of sowing and reaping and encouraged people to give in order to gain personally. What do you learn about this kind of false teaching in Acts 8:14-22?

8. Give some examples of ways this false teaching has made its way through the church.

Reflecting

1. What positive and negative feelings do you have about people raising money for a Christian cause?

2. In 2 Corinthians 9:7 Paul encourages cheerful giving. The word is the root of our English word, *hilarious*. It is the exact opposite of calculated giving under compulsion. According to these two chapters, how could you become a more cheerful giver?

3. What is the connection between love and giving in 1 John 3:17-18?

4. List some practical ways you are giving or can give to advance God's kingdom.

5. Share a time you were on the "receiving" end of someone's generous giving. How did their "gift" point you to God?

6. Look up the word "generous" in a dictionary and write out the definition. List several synonyms. Do these words describe you? Why or why not?

7. What steps can you take today to become a generous giver?

Satan's Disguise

Lesson 8

Read 2 Corinthians chapters 10&11.
Focus on 2 Corinthians 11:13-15.

For such are false apostles, deceitful workers, transforming themselves into apostles of Christ. And no wonder! For Satan himself transforms himself into an angel of light. Therefore it is no great thing if his ministers also transform themselves into ministers of righteousness, whose end will be according to their works.

Lesson Focus - From Deception to Discernment

2 Corinthians 11:14 tells us that "Satan disguises himself as an angel of light," which means that Satan capitalizes on our love of the light in order to deceive. He wants us to think that he is good, truthful, loving, and powerful – all the things that God is. To portray himself as a dark, devilish being with horns would not be very appealing to the majority of people. Most people are not drawn to darkness, but to light. Therefore, Satan appears as a creature of light to draw us to himself and his lies.

How can we discern, therefore, which light is of God and which light is of Satan? Our minds and hearts are easily confused by conflicting messages. How can we make sure we are on the right path? Just as God's voice spoke physical light into existence, it can speak spiritual light into our hearts. Exposure to His voice – in His Word – will help us recognize the difference between the good light of God and that which is counterfeit.

Beholding

Satan presents sin to us as something pleasing and beautiful to be desired, and he presents false teaching as enlightening and life-changing. Millions follow his pied piper songs simply because they do not know God's truth.

Darkness is a result of attempting to find truth without the Word of God. Sadly, as Isaiah says in chapter 8:20-22, when people do not have the "dawn," they wander in darkness and often become angry at God, refusing to come to Him for help. This is why Satan's masquerade as an angel of light is so effective. It turns white to black and black to white and gets us believing that God is the liar, that God is the source of darkness. Then, in our distress, we focus our hatred towards the only One who can save us.

1. It is important to know that though there is a spiritual battle, victory belongs to the believer. What do you learn about victory for the believer in Jesus Christ from the following verses?

   - Deuteronomy 20:4

   - Romans 8:37

   - 1 Corinthians 10:13

   - Ephesians 6:13

   - 1 John 5:4

2. Though Christ has won the victory for every believer, there are many Christians who live in continual defeat. Ephesians 4:27 explains why. Write out the verse in its entirety.

3. What are some ways that Christians can give place to the devil and darkness?

4. Share a time that Satan used a difficulty in your life to cause you to doubt God.

5. What do we learn about light and the Word of God from the following verses?

    - Psalm 119:105

    - Psalm 119:130

    - 2 Peter 1:19

6. In light of the truth found in John 8:44, why is the Word of God one of the most powerful weapons a believer possesses?

7. According to 2 Corinthians 10:5 where does the spiritual battle begin? How does this verse teach us to battle our thought life?

8. *Paul was confident of the Corinthian church, but not all the Corinthians were equally confident of Paul. He was accused of being strong in his letters, but weak in person. His authority and oversight of the church were being challenged by some. Paul teaches us a valuable lesson – he refuses to respond in his flesh. The carnal weapons Paul refuses are not material weapons like swords and spears. The carnal weapons he renounced were the manipulative and deceitful ways his opponents used. Paul would not defend his apostolic credentials with the carnal weapons others might use. (Guzik)*

    Paul recognized that Satan loves to position one believer against another. Give some examples of carnal (fleshly or worldly) weapons that we sometimes use?

9. 2nd Corinthians 10:1 describes the attitude Paul used in handling his discussion with the believers in Corinth. Why is this attitude critical to solving problems with other believers?

10. Paul was forced to respond to the slander from his critics. It is important to note that he is not defending himself, but his ministry and apostolic authority.

    What can we learn from Paul's example in being discerning while dealing with opposition in ministry?

Becoming

1. Read 2 Corinthians 11:1-15 and comment on those verses that point to the deception Paul is concerned about.

2. Read the Phillips translation of 2 Corinthians 11:1-6 to help you grasp this important passage of Scripture.

   I wish you could put up with a little of my foolishness—please try! My jealousy over you is the right sort of jealousy, for in my eyes you are like a fresh unspoiled girl who I am presenting as fiancé to your true husband, Christ himself. I am afraid that your minds may be seduced from a single-hearted devotion to him by the same subtle means that the serpent used towards Eve. For apparently you cheerfully accept a man who comes to you preaching a different Jesus from the one we told you about, and you readily receive a spirit and a Gospel quite different from the ones you originally accepted. Yet I cannot believe I am in the least inferior to these extra-special messengers of yours. Perhaps I am not a polished speaker, but I do know what I am talking about, and both what I am and what I say is pretty familiar to you.

3. Why was Paul jealous for the Corinthian believers?

4. Describe the difference between godly jealously and fleshly jealously.

5. How did the serpent deceive Eve by his craftiness in Genesis 3:1-5?

6. Instead of being naïve and accepting of false teachers, what relevant instruction do we receive in Romans 16:17-19 and Jude 17-21?

7. How did Paul describe the false teachers in 2 Corinthians 11:13-15?

8. The Greek word translated "transforms" in these verses means to "disguise" or "masquerade". It is important to note these false teachers "transformed" themselves into ministers of righteousness. Give an example of how "false teachers" operate among believers today.

9. What are some reasons people fall for the "disguise" of false teachers today?

10. Read 2 Corinthians 11:20. What were the Corinthians "putting up" with in their lack of judgment regarding these deceitful men?

11. Have you fell victim to false teaching or doctrine? Why or why not? List the criteria a believer can use to distinguish between an authentic minister of Christ and a fake. Use Scripture to support your answer.

Reflecting

1. How does the glory of God and the Body of Christ suffer when Christians fight against one another?

2. Read Ephesians 6:10-18 and 2 Timothy 2:3-4. How can you practically apply these victorious truths to your every-day struggles?

3. Share a time you had to share the truth in love with another believer. Were they receptive to your instruction? Why or why not?

4. Read 2 Corinthians 11:22-33. It has been said that Paul's scars were his credentials. List some of the sufferings that Paul endured in the ministry.

5. In addition to the suffering Paul encountered, what gave him most concern in 2 Corinthians 11:28?

6. Ponder Corinthians 11:29 in the Living Bible translation.

   Who makes a mistake and I do not feel his sadness? Who falls without my longing to help him? Who is spiritually hurt without my fury rising against the one who hurt him?

   Based on what you have learned about Paul's concern for the Corinthian church, describe the heart of a shepherd. Use Scripture to support your answer.

7. Look up the word "discernment" in a dictionary and write out a few definitions and synonyms to help you better understand the word.

8. The Corinthian believers were spiritually immature and lacking in discernment. Read Hebrews 5:12-14 and explain why these Christians were unable to spot false teachers and doctrine.

9. On a scale of 1-10 with 10 being very discerning, how would you rate your spiritual discernment?

10. What can you do to grow in spiritual discernment? Use Scripture to support your answer.

The Ministry of the Thorn

Lesson 9

Read 2 Corinthians chapter 12.
Focus on 2 Corinthians 12:7-10.

And lest I should be exalted above measure by the abundance of the revelations, a thorn in the flesh was given to me, a messenger of Satan to buffet me, lest I be exalted above measure. Concerning this thing I pleaded with the Lord three times that it might depart from me. And He said to me, "My grace is sufficient for you, for My strength is made perfect in weakness." Therefore most gladly I will rather boast in my infirmities, that the power of Christ may rest upon me. Therefore I take pleasure in infirmities, in reproaches, in needs, in persecutions, in distresses, for Christ's sake. For when I am weak, then I am strong.

Lesson Focus - From Struggle to Surrender

One Bible scholar aptly described 2 Corinthians 12:7-10 as the "Ministry of the Thorn". There are so many valuable lessons to be gleaned from these verses as we seek to be women who live from glory to glory. Consider the summary of one commentator.

Certainly, because of the surpassing greatness of the revelations Paul had experienced, pride was a constant temptation. Therefore, to keep him humble, Paul was given ... a thorn in the flesh, a messenger of Satan to torment him.

Beholding

1. Describe some of the revelations God had given Paul including his experience in 2 Corinthians 12:1-4.

    - Acts 9:4, 5

    - Acts 18:9, 10

    - Acts 23:11

    - 2 Corinthians 12:1-4

2. Paul revealed God's divine purpose for his thorn in the flesh in 2 Corinthians 12:7. What was it?

3. "Exalted above measure" or "over-exalted" is used only one other time in the New Testament in 2 Thessalonians 2:3-4. How do these verses provide additional insight into what you are learning from 2 Corinthians 12:7?

4. The word used for exalted above measure refers to *the inflating of ego*. The Lord had so blessed Paul that pride was a constant temptation. How can God's goodness to us personally or in ministry present a problem with pride?

5. What are some precautions we can take to avoid pride having its outworking in our lives? Use Scripture to support your answer.

Some Thoughts on the Thorn

"A thorn in the flesh was given to me" – denotes a pointed stake; a splinter; something excruciatingly painful. There is much speculation surrounding the nature of Paul's thorn in the flesh. It has been suggested that it was could have been physical or spiritual, or something to do with his human nature (flesh) that brought pain and distress to Paul.

- *Some say it was a physical in nature, a possible eye affliction, epilepsy, headaches, an intestinal disorder or speech impediment.*
- *John MacArthur, based on Paul's account in 2 Corinthians 11, believes it may have been deceivers sent to seduce the Corinthians into a rebellion against him.*
- *Some think it was mental or spiritual in nature; nagging criticism, nagging doubt, or a persistent temptation.*

- *Martin Luther and John Calvin both thought that one of Satan's emissaries kept on throwing evil suggestions, or fiery darts into his mind. Something indeed that kept Paul on his face before God.*

- *Alan Redpath said it may have been something in his own personal character and life which was constantly reminding him of the sinfulness of the flesh and which ultimately brought him to what he writes in Romans 7, "For I know that in me (that is, in my flesh) nothing good dwells…"*

Because Paul does not identify the thorn for us, all of the above is mere speculation. It is actually more useful that we don't know, because no matter what our suffering may be, we can apply the lessons Paul learned and receive encouragement for our own thorns.

6. Whatever Paul's thorn was, it did not give him an excuse to stop serving the Lord! How might any of the above suggested thorns prevent believers from accomplishing the call of God on their lives?

7. Paul regarded his thorn as caused by Satan but allowed by God and used by God to accomplish an important purpose. Compare this biblical truth with Job 1:6-12.

8. To better understand the "buffeting" of this thorn in Paul's life, look up the definition of the word "buffeting".

9. Consider Alan Redpath's comments on Paul's buffeting by Satan.

   Paul, punched about by the devil? Who would have thought it? "Perhaps you have looked into the face of a Christian who is always smiling, who never seems to have any worry, is always happy and radiant and, as you have thought about your own circumstances, you have said in your heart, 'I wish I were he! He seems to have no problems. He doesn't have to take what I do.' But perhaps you have lived long enough, as I have, to know that sometimes the most radiant face hides great pressures, and often the man who is being most blessed of God is being most buffeted by the devil.

Considering what you have learned so far, is there a thorn that God has allowed in your life? Take a moment to identify it.

Becoming

The goodness of God does not consist in a desire to cushion His children from the hardships and pains of life, but in a providential interest in us…aimed at our moral development.

Hugh Evan Hopkins

God uses suffering as a tool to build godly character in us. Our response to suffering will determine whether or not it will be eternally profitable.

1. Based on 2 Corinthians 12:8, how did Paul respond to his thorn?

2. Compare Jesus in the Garden of Gethsemane in Matthew 26:36-46.

3. What was God's response to both pleas?

4. Describe some of the ways we try to deal with suffering when God allows it in our lives?

5. Paul petitioned the Lord and was overruled by God who knows best, makes no mistakes, and loves us perfectly. God does not always answer our prayers with the removal of our afflictions, but He gives us His grace to endure the suffering so that it works for us and not against us.

   How has God's grace sustained you in times of great difficulty?

6. The ministry of the thorn seeks to make our suffering eternally profitable. Explain how thorns are to practically work out in the following areas of our lives:

    - To reveal our character

    - To humble us

    - To draw us closer to God

    - To allow God to display His grace and power in us

Reflecting

1. Do you believe that God's grace is sufficient? Explain your answer.

2. Practically, how are we sustained and strengthened by the grace of God? Use Scripture to support your answer.

3. Why do we need to keep ourselves in a place of total dependence on God?

4. God did not allow this thorn in the flesh to punish Paul, or to keep him weak for the sake of weakness. God allowed it to show a divine strength in Paul. Share a time that you were surprised by God's strength in your weakness.

Of course, the greatest example of the principle Paul is communicating was lived by Jesus Himself. "Could anyone on earth be more meek than the Son of God to be hung on the cross, hung in our place that He might redeem us from our sins? As that point of absolute weakness was met by the mighty power of God as He raised Him from the dead, I wonder if the pressure of the thorn in Paul's life was a reminder of the power of the cross.

Alan Redpath

5. What did Paul write in Philippians 3:10-11? How did his life demonstrate the power of the cross?

6. How should the truth of the power of the cross practically work in out in our daily walks?

The Danger of Self-Deception

Lesson 10

Read 2 Corinthians chapter 13.
Focus on 2 Corinthians 13:5-6.

Examine yourselves as to whether you are in the faith. Test yourselves. Do you not know yourselves, that Jesus Christ is in you?—unless indeed you are disqualified. But I trust that you will know that we are not disqualified.

Lesson Focus – From Professing to Possessing

Sometimes the truth can be a hard thing to swallow, especially when it means coming to the realization there are things we need to change in our lives. One of the dangerous things about lying is that when people tell the lies long enough they can start to believe they are actually true. The same applies to the lies we tell ourselves. People often deceive themselves to avoid doing those things necessary to confront the truth. False teaching, religious compromise, and personal sin have all found acceptance and even approval in people's lives through the use of self-deception. As the days grow darker, we need to examine ourselves and be sure the Christian life we are professing is the life we are possessing.

Beholding

1. Review 2 Corinthians 12:21. What do we know about the condition of some of the believers in Corinth who professed faith but were living otherwise?

2. Read James 1:22-25. Explain how hearing the word without doing the word can be an act of self-deception.

3. What did Jesus teach in Luke 6:46-49 about the difference between a "doer" of the Word and a "non-doer"?

4. The word “deceiving” in James 1:22 means to *reckon wrong* or to *draw false conclusions*; then to *cheat or deceive by false reasoning*. When we are drawing or coming to false conclusions, we are cheating ourselves of the knowledge and the power of truth, deceiving ourselves.

   How is it easy to believe that we have acted upon something we know to be true, when in reality we have not? Give an example.

5. What are the potential dangers of self-deception in a believer’s life?

6. Why is Paul’s tone so stern 2 Corinthians 13:2?

7. Matthew looks at the role of church discipline presented in Matthew 18:15-17. Describe the order and actions taken in dealing with a sinning brother or sister.

8. Compare Matthew 18:16 with 2 Corinthians 13:1. What do you discover?

9. Where the Corinthian believers were challenging Paul’s authority, he now issues a challenge in 2 Corinthians 13:5. Fill in the blanks.

____________________yourselves as to whether you are in the __________________.

____________________yourselves.

Do you not know yourselves, that ________________ __________________ is in you?

- Unless indeed you are ____.

Becoming

We are often very ready to examine and test others. But first, and always first, we must examine and test ourselves. That was the trouble at Corinth. They criticized Paul and failed to examine themselves.

Alan Redpath

1. Read Psalm 139:23-24. How do these verses help us to better understand what it means to examine ourselves?

2. Alan Redpath provides us with further insight.

   To examine yourself, in fact, is to submit to the examination and scrutiny of Jesus Christ the Lord – and this never to fix attention on sin but on Christ – and to ask Him to reveal that in you which grieves His Spirit; to ask Him to give you grace that it might be put away and cleansed in His precious blood. Self-examination takes the chill away from your soul, it takes the hardness away from your heart, it takes the shadows away from your life, and it sets the prisoner free.

   In light of what you have read, write in your own words what it means to examine and test ourselves to see if we are really in the faith.

3. When we examine ourselves or others, we are looking for Jesus in us! We are not to look for perfection, in ourselves or in others; but we should see real evidence of Jesus Christ in us.

   Examine yourself. What proof do you have that Christ is living in you?

   Henry Morris writes that...

   Paul here reminds the Corinthians--and us--that it is quite possible for a man or woman to profess Christ and salvation, yet still be unsaved. They may even deceive themselves into thinking that such a profession has saved them. Therefore, we need to examine ourselves to prove ourselves. The sure proof is the realization that Christ is indwelling us, by the Holy Spirit, resulting in godly lives and glad acceptance of all the revealed Word of God, as inspired by the same Holy Spirit.

4. The Lord gave Paul authority over the Corinthian church for their edification, not their destruction. Instead of receiving his rebuke, they were offended by it. Look up the word "rebuke" in a dictionary and write out the definition.

5. What do you learn about receiving a rebuke in Proverbs 15:31?

6. Often the Lord will use other believers to chasten us through a sound rebuke. Share a time you were on either the giving or receiving end of a rebuke.

7. What does Hebrews 12:5-6 teach us about the proper motive in a rebuke? Describe from Hebrews 12:11 the purpose of a rebuke.

Reflecting

1. Paul loved the Corinthians and wanted only the best for them. Why is it easy to become defensive when we are called out on our sin?

2. How did Paul model Ephesians 4:29 in his dealing with the sin issues of the church?

3. How can self-examination and an accountability partner protect us from deceiving ourselves?

4. Paul recognized that he was the topic of ungodly conversation among some of the Corinthian believers. In 2 Corinthians 12:20, he mentions contentions, jealousies, outbursts of wrath, selfish ambitions, backbitings, whisperings, conceits and tumults.

   In what ways do we give place to self-deception when we gossip and speak behind someone's back?

5. Take some time to ponder Paul's closing words to the Corinthian church in 2 Corinthians 13:11. Give a practical example of how you might put his instruction immediately to work.

   - Become complete

   - Be of good comfort

   - Be of one mind

   - Live in peace

6. Paul's benediction in 2 Corinthians 13:14 beautifully highlights the Trinity – Father, Son and Holy Spirit and the blessings that are ours because we are children of God. Notice the order: it is through the grace of the Son, our Lord Jesus Christ, that we come to know the love of our Father, God, and experience the communion and fellowship of the Holy Spirit. The word "amen" affirms the blessings to all Christians. As you meditate and ponder these glorious truths, what blessings from God are you especially grateful for today?

7. What personal examples from Paul's ministry to the Corinthians most inspired you?

8. Which lesson in your study of 2 Corinthians has most impacted your Christian walk?

9. What "action" plan will you put in place to be intentional in your desire to move from glory to glory?

About the Author

Margy Hill's passion and calling for women's ministry led her to start the Women's Ministry Connection where she encourages and exhorts women leaders in ministry. God has given her the opportunity to speak into the lives of women of all ages and church backgrounds.

She loves to teach and share her passion for the Word of God to stir women to a deeper and more abundant relationship with Jesus and to encourage and equip them to walk in the fullness of their callings.

Her gift for writing has led her to write several Bible studies to help women develop a desire to dig deeper into the Word of God. With challenging questions and everyday application, her studies have been widely used throughout churches in the United States.

Margy speaks and teaches for women's conferences, retreats and seminars and is also known for her "Hope for the Hurting Heart" training seminars to help equip women to counsel confidently from the Word of God.

Margy resides in Newport News, Virginia and is blessed to be able to serve with her husband who is the "Reaching Around" Pastor at Calvary Chapel Newport News. She loves being a part of the women's ministry team, serving the women in weekly Bible study.

For more information, visit her website at www.wmconnection.org.

Made in the USA
Columbia, SC
27 February 2023

13053567R00041